The Ablation of Time

David Atkinson

The Ablation of Time

Acknowledgements and Thanks

Many of the poems in this collection (some in slightly different form) have appeared in the following publications:
in Australia: *Australian Poetry Collaboration, Eureka Street, FreeXpresSion, The Mozzie, Poetry Matters, Polestar, Positive Words, Quadrant, Short and Twisted, Speed Poets, Tamba.*
in the USA: *Avalon Literary Review, The Avocet, Feelings of the Heart, Poetry Explosion Newsletter, Poets West, Pudding Magazine, Quill and Parchment, Road Not Taken.*

I am grateful to the editors and publishers for their encouragement of poets and their dedication to poetry.

I would like to thank Ron Wilkins for his criticism, guidance and encouragement in many ways. Thanks to Gisela Sophia Nittel, who also commented on many of the draft poems and provided advice. Thanks also to the members of the Harbourside and Eastwood poetry groups for continuing support on the journey through the world of poetry.

My loving appreciation to Judy for her constant support as always.

For Judy

The Ablation of Time
ISBN 978 1 76041 521 1
Copyright © text David Atkinson 2018
Cover photo: Australian Landscape of Tree and Rocks on Hilltop
© Judah

First published 2018 by
GINNINDERRA PRESS
PO Box 3461 Port Adelaide 5015 Australia
www.ginninderrapress.com.au

Contents

Sculpted	7
Immersed	8
Eddies of Memory	9
Resonance	10
An Education From the Crows	11
Freedom From Foresight	12
Villanelle for the Fox Cubs	13
With the Beatles	14
The Ablation of Time	15
Tough Love	16
All is Vanity	17
Awakening	18
A Failed Harvest	19
Identity of the Egret	20
Napoleonic Warfare	21
Stirred by the Strands	22
Segregated	23
Tidal Emotions	24
River Heights	25
A Darting Lorikeet	26
At Con's Café	27
Captured by the Foxes	28
Gloger Observed	29
Highway Annuity	30
Elation As He Soars	31
Apprehended Knowledge	32
Scribbly Gum	33
Remember	34
It's a Long Way	35
The Limits of Comprehension	36

A Poet's Panorama	37
Gypsy Flare	38
Stories of Cars	39
Bypassed	40
The Country of the Soul	41
Nostalgia For Small Things	42
Life on the Edge	43
Authentic Praise	44
The Dress Circle	45
A Strict Pantoum	46
150 Years After	47
Ephemeral Beauty	48
The Hitch-kick Mastered	49
A Second Scene	50
Contrarian	51
Foreshore Torsion	52
Exclusive Eccentricity	53
Adjusting the PC	54
Times Square 11 p.m.	55
Where Whitman Walked	56
A Wilful Child	57
An Explorer's Grand Obsession	58
Father	60
Masked Memory	61
Bleak Perhaps	62
Why Poetry?	63

Sculpted

An arduous chronicle of granite grey hands.
Narrative of knuckles; calloused,
gnarled like a tree trunk
grafted in earlier days.
Distorted joints chiselled, nails chipped
by the stones of the honest earth.

Skin soaked and soiled by engine oil,
seepage of the sump.
The post holes dug,
the tendons and fence wire strained.
Digits cracked and chafed from morning milking,
by absorption of the blood of the beast slaughtered
on the killing tree.
Stain of a slaughterman;
an endurance of skinning,
the odour of gutting.

The laceration, the scrubbing;
a futile battle each night
at the laundry tub.
An existence which cannot be purged
by the ritual of the Solvol.

Immersed

Fly-strike: a parasitic relationship between fly maggots and sheep

Wheeze and cough, saliva drools;
they wheel as one, controlled by fear.
Early morning sheep yards.

The yap and yelp of kelpies,
one eye to the farmer,
one eye to the mob.
Bred for this contest
of unequal wills;
their skill is bravado and bluff.

In hoppers and heat,
the stench of panting wool.
Four-tooths from the river flats;
recalcitrant bleats of docile defiance.
Laconic call 'Come back'.

It's definite, destined; the restless sheep are edged
and urged along the race.

Resistance depleted, almost cowered,
a Corriedale leaps;
its body submerges, the plunger immerses
its head in the dip.

And flies;
the yard vibrates
with a cloud of innumerable flies.

Eddies of Memory

Murray and Darling junction;
river red gum saplings, reeds,
subdued chatter of yellow rosellas.

Deep convergence, silence.
A flashback fifty years;
sitting in a primary class,
remote country town.
Teacher strides. Our great rivers,
highways of the pioneers.

Wooden desk, attached chair;
cramped for a gangly boy.
Initials 'B.T.', a predecessor's etching.
Sunlight dances on last year's
ink spill.

Remnant fragments swirl,
corellas circling on the river.
Recollections flow, the tributaries
of recall; unconscious eddies.

Memory drifts back
like skeins of geese returning
to the river as daylight pales.

Resonance

Remote Cape York Peninsula.
From hollow stringybark the drumming
resounds, elevated.
Potential nesting hole
of the smoky-grey palm cockatoo.

Wispy fly-away crest, regal rouge
cheek patches, the male hammers,
beats a drumstick he has fashioned
for the purpose.
Female scrutinises, the right to veto
the selected site.

Dramatic spectacle of shrieking and bowing,
a piercing call.

Territorial display?
Demonstration of cognitive ability?
Resonance to determine durability
of the cavity?
Monitored for only thirty years,
objective of the striking mystifies.

Unique trait; a tool created
for an enterprise other than eating.
Incessant, the parrot taps
and batters…

An Education From the Crows

In dead trees on the river flats
the satin crows stand sentinel.
They guard the only waterholes
as undertakers who convene
macabre events they now dictate.

Though water is the source of life,
skeletal sheep cannot make haste;
their tracks are parched in scorching haze.
The crows watch in their soulless grace,
each caw a call of need and greed.

Long ago emaciated,
one desperate ewe descends the bank;
she must push through the mud and squelch.
To life-giving cool she stumbles;
an eye is taken, still alive.

On daily rounds we pass a dam;
the crows rip at some new remains.
Reluctant scavengers withdraw,
possessive of today's carrion.
At school we learn of Mr Darwin.

Freedom From Foresight

A cantata soars from the eyrie
in the foliage depths, camouflaged;
two magpies carol
in callistemon harmony.

Throats vibrate, magnolia beaks point skyward,
poised as the batons of conductors.
Lilting duet of the flautists.
To humans, melodious mindfulness.

The descant wavers, and expands.
Prolonged euphonic song.
Liberated from fear, from contemplation
of the inevitability,
the inescapability,
of death.

Villanelle for the Fox Cubs

We found the cubs inside a hollow tree,
such little foxes when I was a boy;
the task to kill the cubs would fall to me.
Protecting lambs the farmer's stern decree.
The greyhound led us there with no decoy;
we found the cubs inside a hollow tree.
The slaughter caused by foxes; all agree
my father's livelihood they would destroy.
The task to kill the cubs would fall to me.
I must ignore their cuteness, that's the key,
and choose the method I might best employ.
We found the cubs inside a hollow tree.
No chance to vacillate, I cannot flee;
to be a man sometimes does not bring joy.
The task to kill the cubs would fall to me.
A massacre by foxes on a spree;
they seemed to slay at random and enjoy.
We found the cubs inside a hollow tree;
the task to kill the cubs would fall to me.

With the Beatles

A meditation Epping Road,
it's a careless Saturday.
CD by The Beatles, fresh-faced
boys in suits sing, 'It Won't
Be Long'; in the moment
for the music and for me.

Transported back the fifty years.
Simplicity, a time of hope,
the yearning of clearer days
when music was the explanation
to doubts there was no need to have.

Immersed in harmonies, guitar
chords fill my space.
Wherever I'm going, absorbed,
it won't be long, as I drive
With the Beatles.*

---

* *With the Beatles* was the second studio album by the Beatles; it was released in November 1963.

The Ablation of Time

At close range the clash
of a cloudburst lapses
in an instant.

Trussed up like bulging penguins,
we huff, our breath freezing on our faces.
Belittled as krill by the blue bolt glacier,
one mile wide,
as it enters the ocean.

Novice glaciologists analyse the rifts
and the stretched crevasses,
cavities in the body of serrated ice
held only by tensile strength.

The crowd murmurs, anticipates the spectacle,
the sonorous drumfire, of ice ablation.
An observer predicts, with conviction,
that any minute a precarious slab, angular,
will break loose and collapse.
Ecstasy for the enthusiasts.

An hour later, spectators grow listless.
It seems that, with *débutant* reluctance, ice calves
not to the minute but to the chronicle
of the ages.

Tough Love

The downy youngster begs and squeals;
bald eagles stare, detached,
scholarly scrutineers.
Blanched silk heads, a regal postage stamp
silhouetted against the Alaskan sky.

Lemon ceres, fish-hooked beaks delineated.
They ply their vicious talons, tradesman's pliers;
opportunistic feeders in the mirror
of the lake expanse.

Posing a parental examination.
Eaglet rehearses, trial of flapping.
Coerced by hunger, risks a precarious flight
to fetid fish posted with care high on a bough
in the old-growth conifer.

All parents understand the value
of an exacting education.

All is Vanity

In the aquarium I stare only at the jellyfish,
backlit and luminous, pale and frail
gossamer veils in suspended inanimation.

Appearing to vacillate,
their existence precarious.
Invertebrate opaque drifters,
they cannot hide from predators;
yet, though 96% water, they have prevailed
since eras long before the age of the dinosaurs.

Reliant on ocelli for simple sight,
on their sensory rhopalia
and on statocysts
to maintain flowing balance.

Other species preen and strut.
But for jellyfish, all tentacles and trails,
no showmanship, no prancing.
Radiant diffidence,
their beauty all the greater
that they are unaware of it.

Awakening

Teenager's first 45, newly-pressed.
He strokes the sleek seductive grooves,
its roundness, raciness.

Vivid voyage on the vinyl.
Emotions energised, he spins.
Youthful senses swirl,
spirits revolve, evolve.
Mesmerised by the music,
he is sliced by its scythe
to the psyche.

The yearnings of youth;
for electric guitars,
delinquent as the back alley,
for dishevelled hair,
even for imagined girls,
elusive and ethereal.
Prohibited cravings stirred,
sharp like the stereo stylus.

A Failed Harvest

Fiery wind jumps
in spindly lifeless grass,
a rusted wire fence.

The aftertaste of dust.
Raw earth compacted
by a history of harvest trucks.
Disused railway line; wheat silo tower;
symbols of a dying town.

Flannelette-shirted, a wiry teenager, purposeful.
He scuffs the laneway from the pub,
redundant abattoir worker.
Resonance of rhythmic bounces;
football handed down by the last brother
gone to work in the city.

Rhythmic bounces. Chaos in the concrete silo
of the mind, stockpile of a failed harvest.
Thoughts convulse as frenzied chaff
on a fitful gust.
A kick at the ruins of the mechanical auger.

The road is parched
in summer haze.

The tartaric taste of tears.
Pauses, hands resolute.
Commences his wretched climb from the plinth
up the solitary silo ladder.

Identity of the Egret

Wades near the foreshore,
estuarine mudflats;
straight and statuesque.
May be a little egret;
erect, motionless.

But, almost sunshine bill,
perhaps a cattle egret;
conceivable, away
from his beast.

Forages, arches his neck;
intermediate egret, non-breeding plumage.

Or an eastern great,
pink lace upper legs.

Late afternoon sun,
gunmetal beak tip;
eastern reef egret.

A species of heron; upright,
exquisite. In his hide,
bird watcher draws breath,
elated; sufficient
to be an egret.

Napoleonic Warfare

The summer stubble slumps
as straw in the heat and haze
of the Eighty Acres.

Massed divisions swarm across the open expanse.
Unlimited reinforcements, ever more troops surge.
Battalions gain and hold hard-won territory.

Strategies exploited for three hundred
million years of expeditionary campaigns.
Jump long distances, stridulate
with reconnaissance parties at the front line,
catapult forward, outflank defences
like outriders beyond the fence wire.

No evolution of battle tactics here.
With a life expectancy of five months,
no trenches to be excavated,
no fear of stalemate or of a pile of corpses,
putrid in the midday sun.

Victory accomplished, inevitable, for the infantry
of the pastures. After the advance
of the grasshoppers, the earth withered,
ravaged now as a no-man's-land.

Stirred by the Strands

Fibres of wool, entangled.
Strands of nostalgia
in the barbed wire fence.

Square-faced wethers complain, yarded
at sunset, dawn shearing.
Dissident confronts the farmer,
stomps its defiance.
Kelpie slavering, silent at last,
slinks off for the shade.

Lustrous fleece, early light
luminous, flung across the classing table,
billows.
Lanolin lacerates, fingers
serrate and sting.
Crimpy Corriedale, strong 'FAQ'.
Skirtings collected, the gang's rouseabout.

Shreds and fibres,
threads of recall.

Segregated

The kangaroos keep silent watch;
they do not need to understand.
The grass is parched
in summer heat beyond the fence.

In death all enter through the gate
for burial;
the townies and the cockies too
arrive by black maria.

The funeral plan is organised;
the undertaker understands.
The digger knows
which graves are to the east,
which graves are to the west,
though diggers are agnostic.

Now Mr Ross and Mr Ryan
will never reconcile;
and hawks will soar above the hill
while gum trees wither in the drought
beside them all.

Tidal Emotions

Despondent and discouraged
when the tide runs out;
sucked dry.
The sun bleaches the barren spirit,
resourceless and exposed
to life's rigours and trials.

On a bright day
the tide rises
on an incoming swell.
A trickle then a torrent
surges and overwhelms
the sediments and impediments
of life.

The tide advances and recedes,
rises and falls,
unceasingly.

River Heights

Dad will be home at ten-to-twelve
for his lunch and the *Country Hour*.
Work boots and flies at the screen door,
glancing eye to the temperature,
cold mutton sandwich from the safe.

We must be quiet so Dad can know
the wool price and 'the state of things'.
Attention to the Bakelite
loud in the corner; we absorb
'the prices of commodities'.

Any rain for the South West Slopes?
The rate for a bushel of wheat.
Fat lambs and heifers in the sale yards
at Wagga and Wodonga;
and the Murray and Murrumbidgee
river heights.

A Darting Lorikeet

A poem is a lorikeet,
a darting rainbow lorikeet;
it seizes the advantage,
then slips and flits away.

A poem flashes in and out,
an early morning wonder;
it squabbles for attention
in the foliage of the mind.

Resourceful and yet restless,
a poem jigs with death;
it dances on the highest wires,
electric inspiration.

A poem stares the poet down,
a calm ingratiation;
it creeps along the dangling bough,
inquisitive free verse.

A poem is a lorikeet;
it screams and screeches allegory,
demanding to be heard.

At Con's Café

A pot of tea for Mrs Hill,
the reek of frying chips;
the muted throb of ceiling fans
to stir the heat and plastic strips
to ward away the languid flies.

A station worker ambles in;
a double-chocolate, double-malt.
I watch a milkshake made
the way they do
in country towns.

The Seekers singing 'Georgy Girl';
the jukebox stands behind the kids
who lounge at booths
of laminated grease.
The social hub of town.

No menu needed, Con appears;
an apron cloaks his mammoth frame.
To take my order – eggs or steak
or steak and eggs,
if that's what you'd prefer.

At breakfast in a country town,
there's time to ponder life.
In mirrors on both sides I see
my infinite reflections.

Captured by the Foxes

A white Arctic fox,
its head slumped,
and almost invisible,
except for its neck and torso,
blood red against the snow.

The white fox hangs lifeless
in the jaws of its biological 'cousin',
the red fox,
its competitor and predator.

Confronted that the graphic picture
is so shocking, complete.
And at last an understanding
of why many human cultures believe
that a photograph
seizes the being.

The prize-winning photograph of the foxes appeared in the *Sydney Morning Herald*.

Gloger Observed

Crimson rosellas forage,
flit among the foliage.
Chatter and dazzle
of amaranth and sapphire.
Bird-watchers hike the coastal heath.

On grazing plains,
remote on the desert margin,
rosellas prattle in the crystal air.
Yellow rosellas; sandy, seared.
Red pigment discarded,
crimson transformed.
As if they have absorbed
the scorched pasture's withered straw.

Birds observe the rule,
twitchers observe the birds.
Elated that an avian species
on a southern continent would conform
to the early nineteenth century theory
of a German zoologist.

Gloger's Rule (1833): dark pigments increase in races of birds living in humid habitats.

Highway Annuity

Cocooned motorist dazzled. Tiered planter boxes swathed
in cerise, draped in magenta, mauve. Luminous blooms, each quivers
on the breeze.

Fifty years from propagation, rumination
of two nurserymen; reflection on fragility,
transience. Each year their famed
azalea blossoms decimated
by the first spring shower,
short-lived petals shrivelled
to slush. Aged painters tortured
by their ephemeral art.

But as the decades slide
the driver grasps his annual gift,
embraces the September annuity
of the old masters.

Elation As He Soars

A young child learns the joy of verse
as a young bird learns to fly.
At first it flutters from the nest
and shrinks against the sky.

Then impulse and instruction bring
to mother on the branch.
With nature, nurture, instinct strong,
the nestling takes the chance.

The child then learns the joy of words
to read and write and more.
To freedom as the bird takes flight,
elation as he soars.

Apprehended Knowledge

Blaze combustion by harvester friction,
mechanical ignition in summer stubble.
A single spark struck on a day
of searing heat.

Furphy tanks on makeshift fire trucks;
lumbering beasts lurch
from neighbouring farms.
Flurries of flame flare
at men disorientated,
aimless ants in the acrid
gunmetal smoke and grit.

A wall of sensate fire flashes,
forked wind shifts scream,
stampede the vaulting
stand of trees.

Last thoughts. All farmers know
you cannot mix fire
with vaporised eucalyptus oil.

Scribbly Gum

Scribbly gum and gnarly,
as with an old man's hand.
Branches angular, arbitrary;
a pattern, but not planned.

Shaded white on slate sky,
moves against the clouds.
Blue bolt water rippled,
wired leaves amongst the shrouds.

A rainbow flash of lorikeet,
galahs upon the bark.
Restless and yet peaceful.
On surface water, stark.

Kaleidoscope of colour
highlights the ghostly tree.
Shimmers on sheer silver.
No purpose but to be.

Remember

I
I remember
I remember learning
I remember learning that
I remember learning that you
I remember learning that you had
I remember learning that you had died.

It's a Long Way

Incessant drilling
industrial hammering
inside my head;
grateful for the ear plugs.
Remember to suggest
to local heavy metal band
addition of a jackhammer.
Note to self: write a poem on noise
in the modern urban environment.
You must stay completely still.
Claustrophobia,
life in a cylinder.
Now I am moving at last,
sitting up.
'Okay, you can get dressed now,
your MRI is done.'

The Limits of Comprehension

To scan the breadth of the cosmos
is to speculate on the immensity
of the universe.

Awed that our sun, hot plasma,
generates the energy we need for life.
One of two hundred billion stars blazing
in the spiral constellation
known as the Milky Way.
Or it might be four hundred billion
flares hurtling.
Out there.

Overwhelmed by the two hundred
billion galaxies, each consisting of perhaps
a hundred billion stars.
Peering out searching for the most distant of them
thirteen billion light years away.

Knowledge acquired; yet
I do not understand
the beauty of the lily or of the dawn sun
on the early wave.

A Poet's Panorama

He paints a panorama,
the pen a brush of words.
To sketch the visual vista
of colour and obsession
and of ambiguity.

The poet's imagination is the easel
of remembering.
From palette to the canvas,
he applies the paint of passion
and bleaches out his brain.

There's inspiration on a good day,
there's texture light and lean.
Lust for landscaped illusion,
for the bee upon the blossom
and the vehemence of the Dutchman's starry night.

Gypsy Flare

Cirrus oscillates, cerise sweeps
through streaks of ochre.
Sun subsides, flamenco dancers swirl.

Suitor and his senorita
strut, ruffle-skirted passion,
silent lace above the river.
Horizon's flames yearn.

Last strands stamp the magenta
baile, primitive cry
beyond the senses.
The revue culminates, a catharsis.
Afterglow; it's twilight.

Stories of Cars

for Harry Chapin 1942–1981

A troubadour laments,
caresses his acoustic guitar.
Epic narratives related in song.
Minstrel with *a crazy dream*
to just drive off in his car.

Fragments of everyday lives
stripped bare, plucked.
Of learning to act,
of ambitions to fly.
Audience sighs to the balladeer's tales
of a 'Taxi'
and of its 'Sequel'.

On the Long Island Expressway the stench
of gasoline and a crumpled wreck
swallowed up in flames.

Bypassed

On approach from the north
the view is of poplars and elms
lining the surrounds
of the town.

The highway banks to the right;
this is new.
Once the route was so familiar;
the cemetery has appeared
on the left.

From the new road
there is a detour into town
for those wanting
petrol or a meat pie.

The government has announced its hopes
the town will not die;
with the new highway,
the trip to the city
is five minutes shorter.

The Country of the Soul

In the scrub and brush of an inner life
there are many seasons.
The country of my consciousness.

In times of drought the barren self
lies fallow in the dust and sand;
the hopelessness of parched plains.

The summer sun of the restless soul
lies listless in the heat waves,
in the anguish of silent screams.

Then through the gloom the clouds advance;
the hope of a savage storm
of sweet release.

Now drizzle in the stifling air,
at first a trickle. Relief of the long
dry creek bed of my being.

And finally the deluge of
growth and creativity;
the long sought harvest of the spirit.

Nostalgia For Small Things

To sleep on the veranda as a child
at the end of a hot summer day…

To drive the truck at age eight
in order to feed grain during the drought…

To contemplate a quarter brick held on the ice of the dam
at noon on a sunny winter's day…

To load up wild pumpkins onto the jeep
in the late afterglow…

To ride a horse past a barbed-wire fence
with no room left for a child's leg…

To yabby in the dam and search for the shadow of black
near the water surface…

To drive to a gate in a ute
with no brakes…

Minor memories; sometimes nostalgia is for
the small things.

Life on the Edge

Late afternoon sun
west of Nyngan
my foot steady
on the accelerator.

In the distance ahead
the eagle wheels, swoops
and descends
onto
the
kangaroo
carcass.

The wedge-tail is larger now;
it dances, bounces,
retreats from the road
as we flash past.

I watch the rear vision.
The wedge-tail returns;
I am surprised
by my fervent hope
he does not become
yet more roadkill.

Authentic Praise

Profile angular, intense,
immersed in the music.
Arms and fingers beating time.

We cannot know how much
he comprehends; for him, engaged
with the organ, this is praise.

His mouth contorts;
his mother sings;
we all sing.
His body, his hands and his fingers sing.

The Dress Circle

My eye is to the Opera House
from here above the sandstone crags.
A passing river-cat below
appears to flow as though in tune.
An early winter afternoon.

No wind or cloud, a token swell,
the picture postcard of the bridge.
I take in Sydney Harbour's blaze,
the sky and water every blue,
dress circle for the favoured few.

The blossom on the banksia
cocoons me in my shades of green.
The modern skyline; I evade
the building work and all that's new,
the excess of Barangaroo.

Our history sadly ebbs away,
the working harbour of romance,
the memory tugboats in my mind.
A scenic waterway for all,
oasis in our urban sprawl.

They cannot take away the view,
they cannot build inside my mind.
With nature at the city's heart,
the pulse of Sydney; I observe
the vista from Ball's Head Reserve.

A Strict Pantoum

What joy to write a strict pantoum,
its rhyming scheme so true and tight.
The structure leaves no elbow room,
a pantoum is perverse delight.

Its rhyming scheme so true and tight,
with rhythm like a tolling bell.
A pantoum is perverse delight,
the form hypnotic as a spell.

With rhythm like a tolling bell,
an ancient style no more in use.
The form hypnotic as a spell,
a new pantoum can still seduce.

An ancient style no more in use,
the structure leaves no elbow room.
A new pantoum can still seduce;
what joy to write a strict pantoum.

150 Years After

The tinkle of the flawless chiming notes
among the trees along the gully floor.
Through dappled shade orchestral music floats;
at least a hundred bellbirds maybe more.
Like choristers upon the whispered breeze,
percussion symphony of ringing sound;
they dart throughout the canopy of trees,
they seem to own the scrubland all around.
The bush then drowses as the night draws near,
when early evening light begins to wane;
their calls to fade away and disappear
till only hidden silence will remain.
And those who think that Kendall said it all
have never walked absorbed in bellbirds' call.

Ephemeral Beauty

The subtle scent approaches chaste perfume,
frail blossoms by the thousand touch my soul.
I stare as for the first time at one bloom,
each petal flawless style and fine control;
I savour each component of the whole.

The breeze becomes a wind and then a shower;
exposed azalea blooms are vulnerable.
The slightest stress plays havoc with each flower.
Now painful petals wither as they fall;
all beauty's fragile and ephemeral.

The Hitch-kick Mastered

On edge as he rehearses what's to come,
immobile at his mark upon the track.
He's single-minded now, fears overcome;
legs pump, explosive speed, no turning back.
Involuntary; so many times he's soared,
his instinct an expression of technique.
The method honed, in rhythm to the board;
hips low, eyes high, he gathers for the leap.
And then a model landing in the sand;
accomplished, disciplined and yet carefree.
Each element precisely as was planned;
his practised long jump style and artistry.
The hitch-kick mastered, perfect execution,
a complex skill; and after, quiet elation.

A Second Scene

Spring Frost, Elioth Gruner (1919), Art Gallery of New South Wales

A herd of dairy cows;
a rustic scene
in early morning light.

The farmer stands in coat and cap
against the cold.
The trees obscure the rising sun;
the glow conveyed in sky and scrub alone.

The interplay of shadows, light,
an ambience of light and tone;
the light, always the light.

And now I see a second scene:
it's early morning Emu Plains.
A man is seated sunrise crisp;
his legs are draped in hessian bags
to ward away the frost.

With dew-wet feet, the artist
paints, his frozen fingers bring
the oil to canvas.

A second scene, a pastoral scene;
a man who paints, obsessed
by early morning light.

Contrarian

Evening, when the quiet east flushes faintly at the sun's last look,
Tom Roberts (c. 1887), National Gallery of Victoria

Still silence of dusk, smell of fresh paint.
Fervent men, bearded, *en plein air* in remnant scrub,
an artists' camp Box Hill.

One stands apart, turns away from the sunset,
stares to the east, clutches his easel.
Absorbs the warm pastoral light,
engulfed by delicate mauve,
the eastern afterglow.

A symbolist romantic,
he gambles;
a venture beyond conformity.
The converse, perverse;
a contrarian.

And, at day's end,
on the canvas he catches
the nocturne, captures
the subtle flush
of twilight.

'Roberts was the first to point out the exquisite and delicate variation in colour and tone of the eastern sky at sunset' – Arthur Streeton (much later).

Foreshore Torsion

Port Jackson fig tree (1934), pencil on paper, Lloyd Rees, collection of University of Queensland

A single sheet of ink drawing paper;
2B pencil lines, silhouette framed.
Tree's textual tension,
throbs; muscular contraction.

Storm-shattered trunk,
blind to the harbour behind.
Foliage imagined, discarded;
yet weeps.
Spawned by a supple eye.

Composition absorbed, technique mastered.
In the words of the artist,
three years of painting with a pencil.

Outline from the point,
bleeds from the side, ethereal.
Depth of shade on shades.

Colour creates character,
they say; impulsive error.
Concealed torsion of timber,
and of lead-stained finger;
imagination fired by a
sharp fine graphite.

Exclusive Eccentricity

A pleasing swish, unwelcome scratch,
my hand creating loops and curls.
This gleaming ancient implement;
my fountain pen, poised and alert,
reflects my essence and my fate.

The curves and strokes across the page,
the cursive lines and stanzas too,
project my voice, reflect my soul,
my act of love as I produce
my inmost hopes, my purging fears.

The frisson as I work in ink,
disaster never far away.
Creative physicality;
for I can press with art and skill.
Exclusive eccentricity.

For those who only sit and type
will never know such intimacy;
you breast today's satanic mills.
My mighty humble fountain pen,
it makes me man and not machine.

Adjusting the PC

'And here, in Age, I feel the need
Of some divining colander
To hold the best of all since done
And let the rest slip through.'
– Rosemary Dobson, 'Divining Colander'

Reviewing life this seems the time
to tidy the PC.
To reassess my memories,
to rename and to clean up,
to manage my account.

So many messages retained,
an overflowing system.
All downloaded, contacts flagged,
lacking space for input
as I labour with my in-box.

Renaming will not be enough
nor storing in the cloud.
Preview, review, press reply.
Need to embrace and rectify,
to comprehend and put to rights.

Personal update, memories
reconciled, adjusted.
Removed the drafts;
to deal with junk I'd like
to simply press delete.

Times Square 11 p.m.

The theatre crowd cannot go home,
for them there is no rush.
Bustled, buoyed and jostled.

Neon billboards pulsate, soar;
but we are addicts,
there is no escape.

Fifth Avenue flows bright yellow
with cabs,
invades my nostrils,
the glamour and grit.

The theatre commences
when the play ends.
With senses overloaded
at the crossroads
of the world,
why would I sleep?

Where Whitman Walked

'And you that shall cross from shore to shore years hence are more to me, and more in my meditations, than you might suppose.'
– 'Crossing Brooklyn Ferry', Walt Whitman (1856)

We walk to Brooklyn Bridge
from downtown.
As I absorb the East River
I imagine the life of the poet
all those years ago.

From our walkway high on the bridge
the sun sparkles on the river below,
the breeze plays quietly
with steel cables and ropes.
New Yorkers jog past, oblivious,
as we breathe the skyline of the city.
All the way to Staten Island
and the Statue of Liberty.

The poet never saw the bridge;
no Empire State, no Liberty.
And yet we see what Whitman saw,
we walk where Whitman walked.

A Wilful Child

A poem is a wilful child;
an overbearing child,
a poem urges like an urchin.

A poem skylarks, jokes;
it pokes you in the eye with glee.
The torment of the bloodshot eye.

A poem acts immature;
it dresses up,
performs a sullen sulk.
An exhausted infant,
a poem will not be controlled.

At times a poem schemes;
tender and cuddly, it comes
on the verge of sleep.
Withdraws, but reappears and grizzles;
the early morning.

A poem bolts away, absconds,
the time you hope
to groom and tidy it.
Emerges bedraggled,
wet hair and dirty cheeks.

A poem is a wilful child; it plays
a game of hide and seek.

An Explorer's Grand Obsession

In a ceaseless sea of ceaseless sand
he staggered blindly on;
a race for pride and glory yet.
Through spinifex, stone and sandhill,
he must not bend his will.

John McDouall Stuart
set out like Burke and Wills
to be the first from south to north;
to travel through the centre dry,
his passion to the gulf or die.

He tried, retreated, tried again,
a magnificent compulsion
to cross two thousand desert miles.
He'd die of thirst or by his hand;
furnace serrating scrub and sand.

His company loyal and pitiful
crossed pitiless salt pans,
phantom gum trees in creek beds.
They ate their camels and their horses
in long-dry water courses.

An endless search for water
and shade; in their delirium
they sought the elusive gorges.
Mirage of red rocks rising
with bush flies and ants feasting.

His tragic rivals beat him north,
his face was gaunt and lean.
Nor did he long survive them;
from his suffering and privation,
this explorer's grand obsession.

In 1861, John McDouall Stuart's party left Adelaide on his sixth expedition. The previous year, Burke and Wills had set out from Melbourne. Both expeditions sought to be the first to cross the arid continent of Australia from south to north.

Father

An eye to the roving distance,
the farmer with flies on his back.
He's a physical man middle-aged;
he bends forward slightly with pain.
Relief will come only from rain.

He's bringing the sheep in for shearing,
the boss with the men in the dust;
he's with them but not really of them.
With circling dogs in the heat,
a blurring of fleeces and feet.

Now is the season for ploughing,
a race to sow seed in the ground,
the continuous pulse of the tractor.
The child sleeps the innocent night,
caring not for the throb or the light.

An undisguised man of the country,
resistant to frost and to fire.
Whether feeding, dipping or stripping,
the essence of rural ritual,
always muscular, spiritual.

Masked Memory

for Kathleen (1920–1968)

To catch the idea of air
in the January heat,
we children escape to the veranda.
Enclosed by wire gauze, a safe
to banish the mosquitos.
The country night hums
a cricket sonata.

My cough hacks the stillness,
I wheeze from the oat dust;
a child should not lark
in the grain silo.

You perch on my bunk,
cradle my head,
your voice sol-fa soft.
You understand shortness of breath,
you say.

My memory specific; the tube is a link,
a line to the tank
and the oxygen mask stretches
across your face,
pallid-pale on the pillow.

Bleak Perhaps

Bleak perhaps, and yet a comfort,
mist and wind and drizzle.
The road is wet and up we go,
the breathing heavy in the coats
and muffled water in our faces.

The sweep of ocean view ahead,
gunmetal sea and rolling
tranquil lake ripples, laps.
Companionable, away from cares.
A few hours can achieve so much,
even joy perhaps.

Why Poetry?

Why poetry, he said,
and why not prose?
Many stories to be told
and 'literary fiction' to be written.

But so much discipline as well,
days and nights obsessing.
A love of language to be sure;
life to be lived instead.

Already forty years of toil,
of discipline and effort,
of early starts and tired days.
Why do that in retirement?

Live in the present, live today,
live fully and alive.
Enjoy it all, be sensitive
with feelings on the surface.

So poetry for me's the thing,
emotions in an hour.
The beauty of the language too,
if selfish, in the moment.

Why poetry?
Intensity.

www.ingramcontent.com/pod-product-compliance
Lightning Source LLC
Chambersburg PA
CBHW062201100526
44589CB00014B/1901